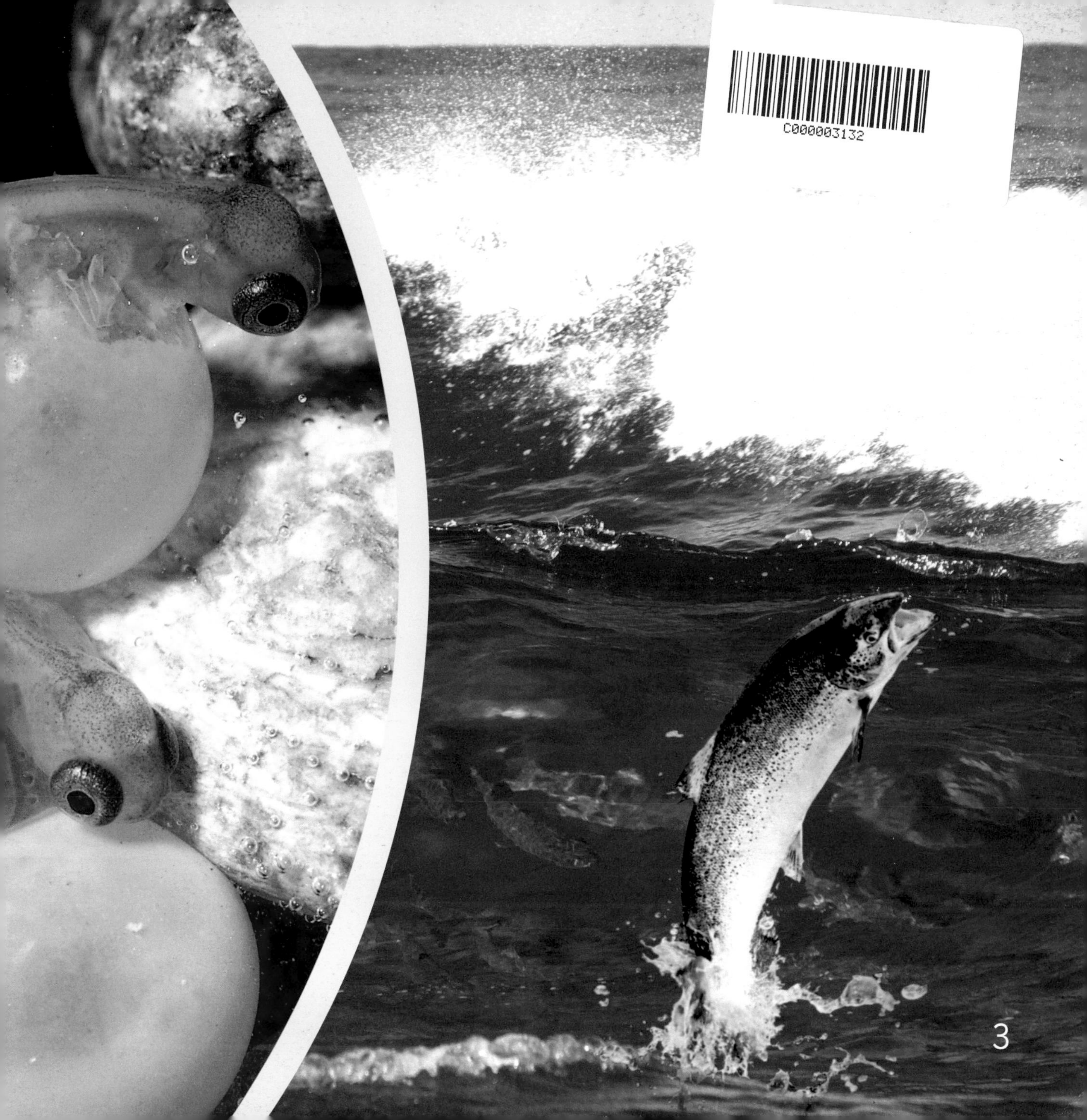

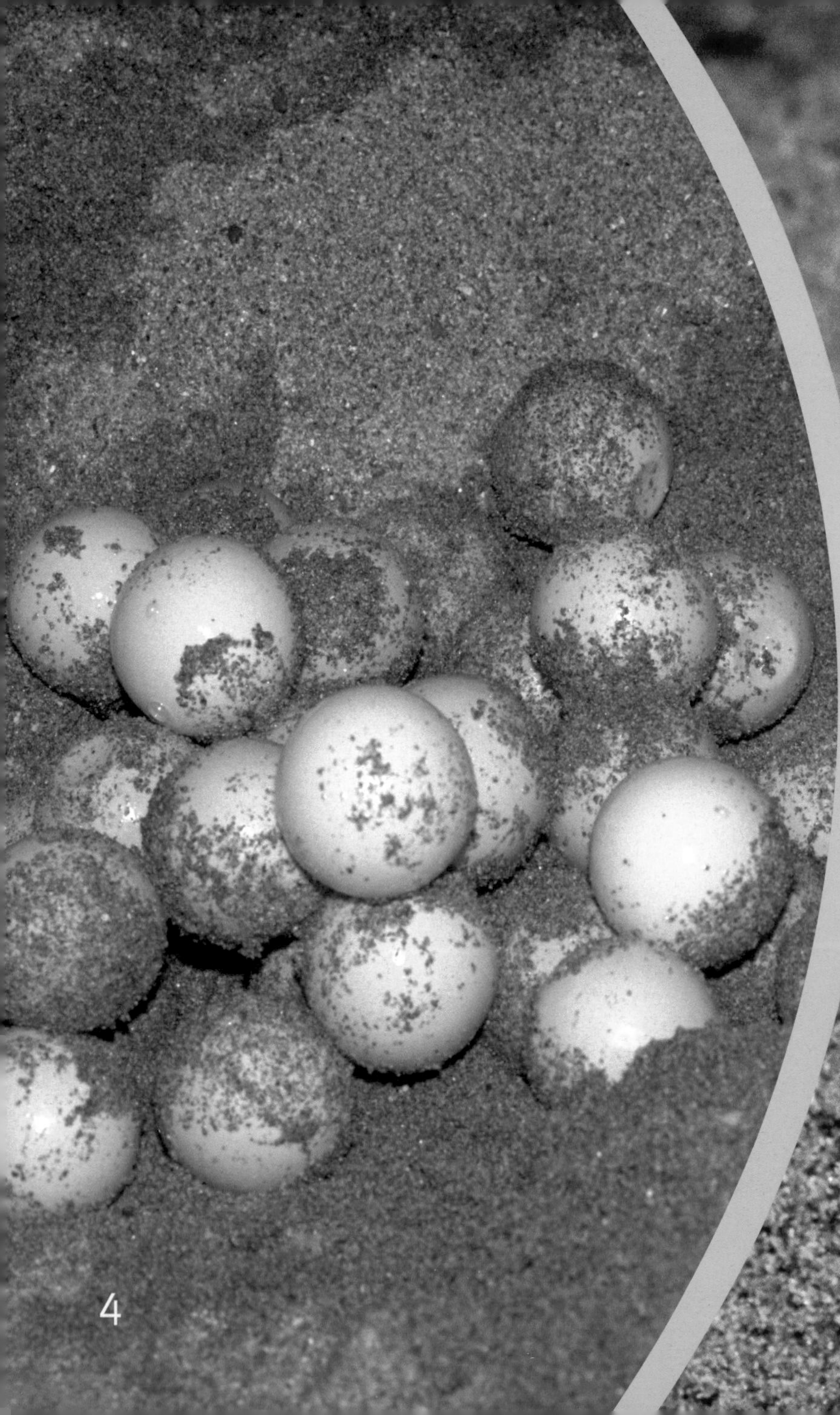
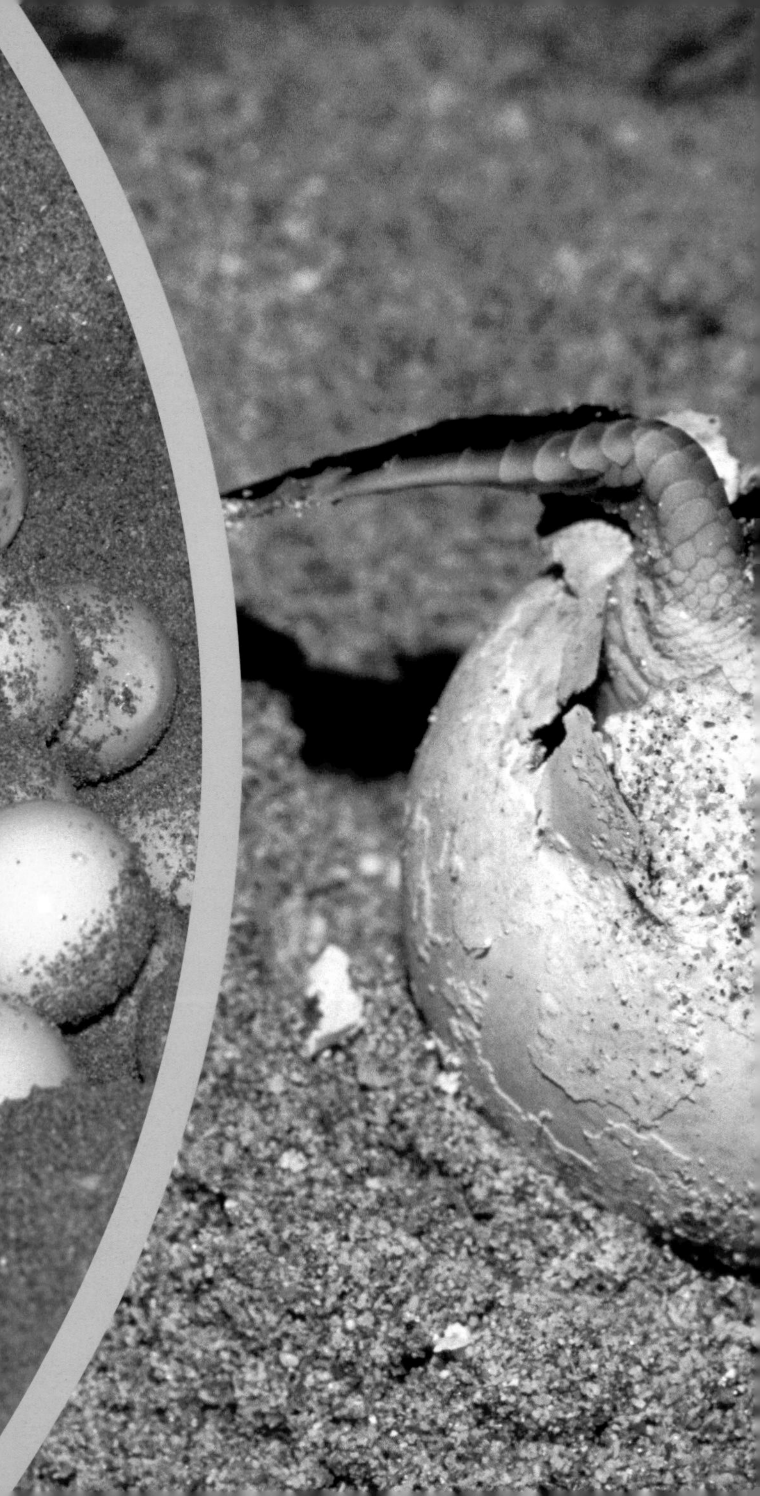

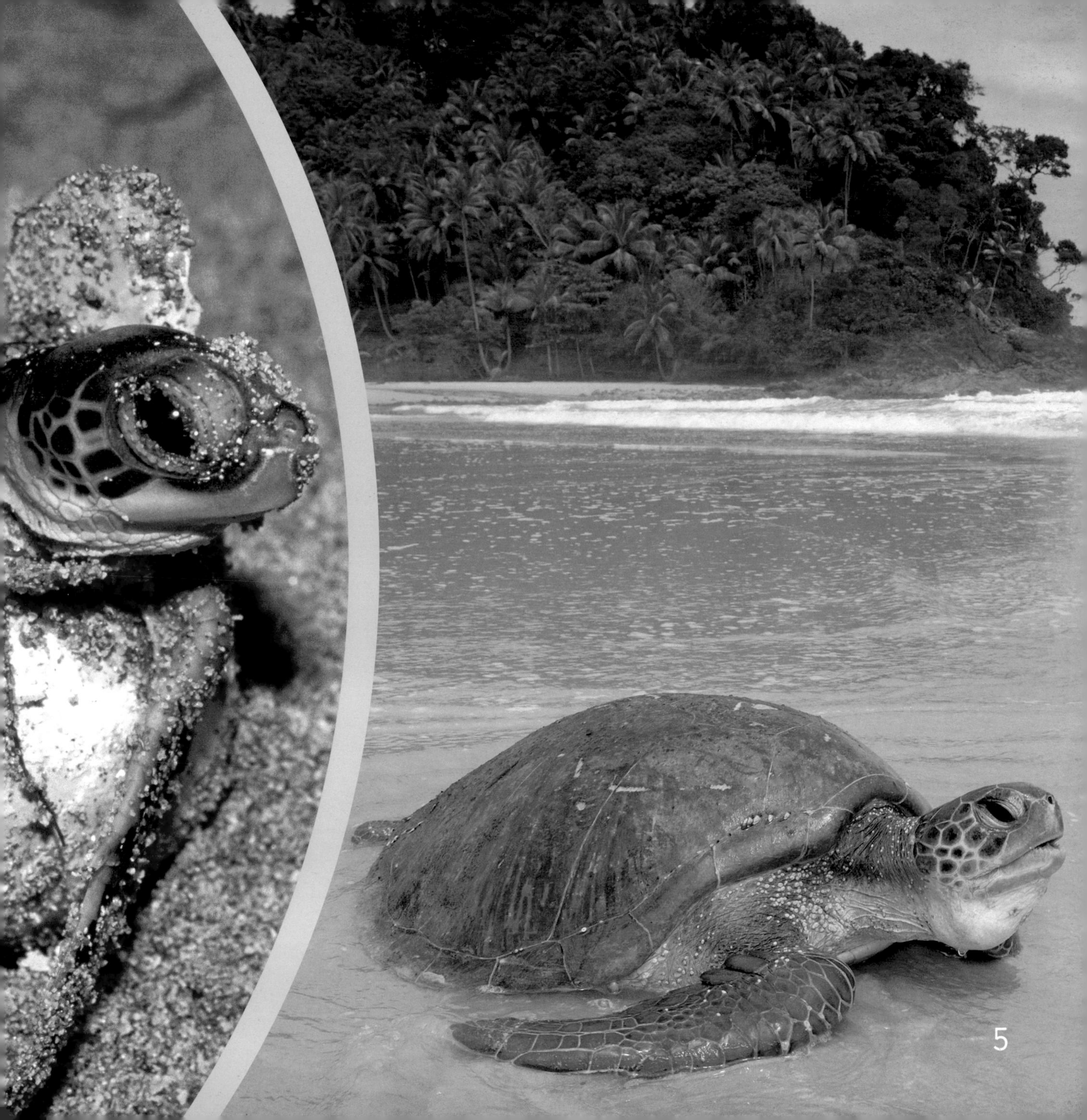

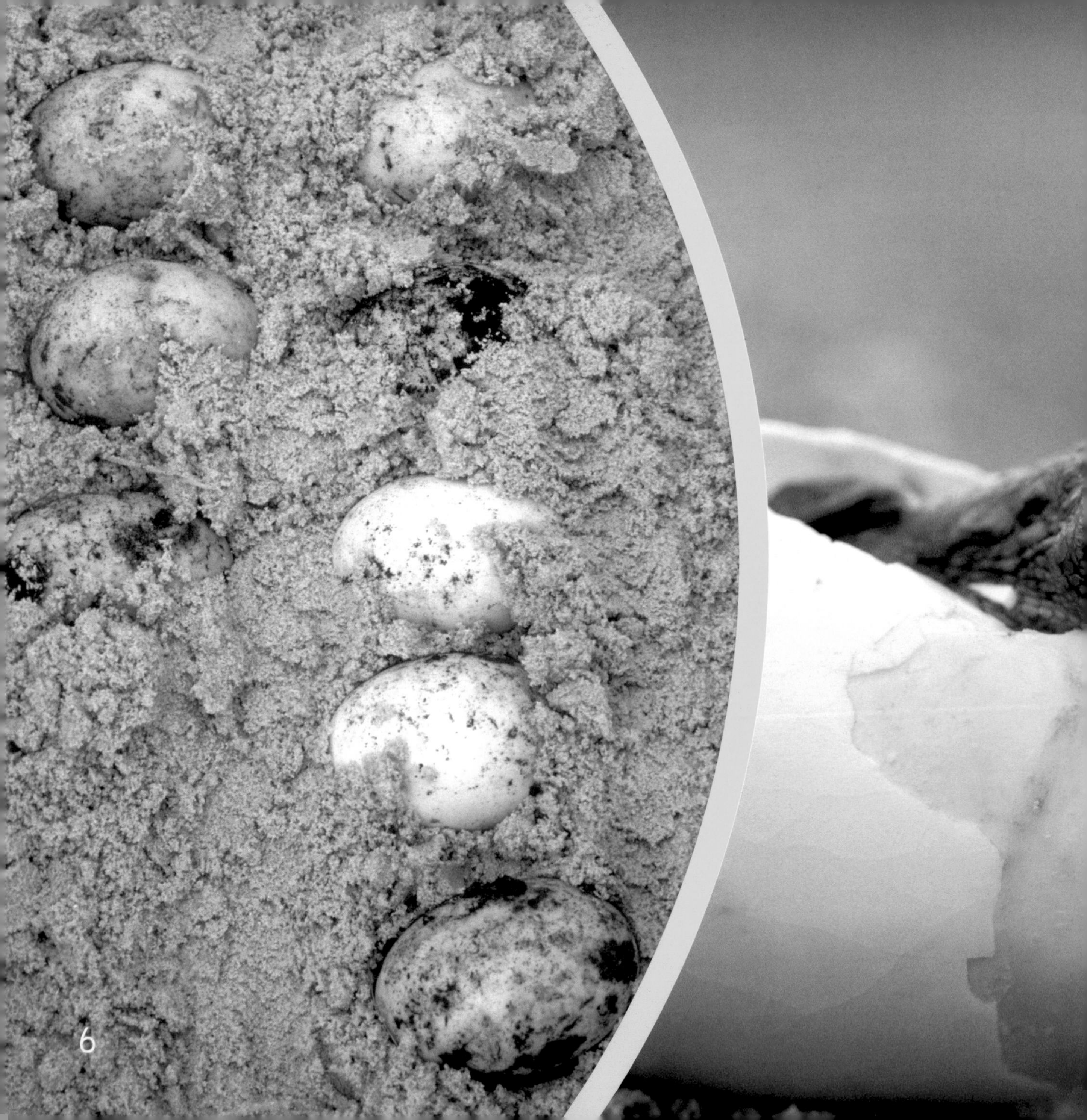

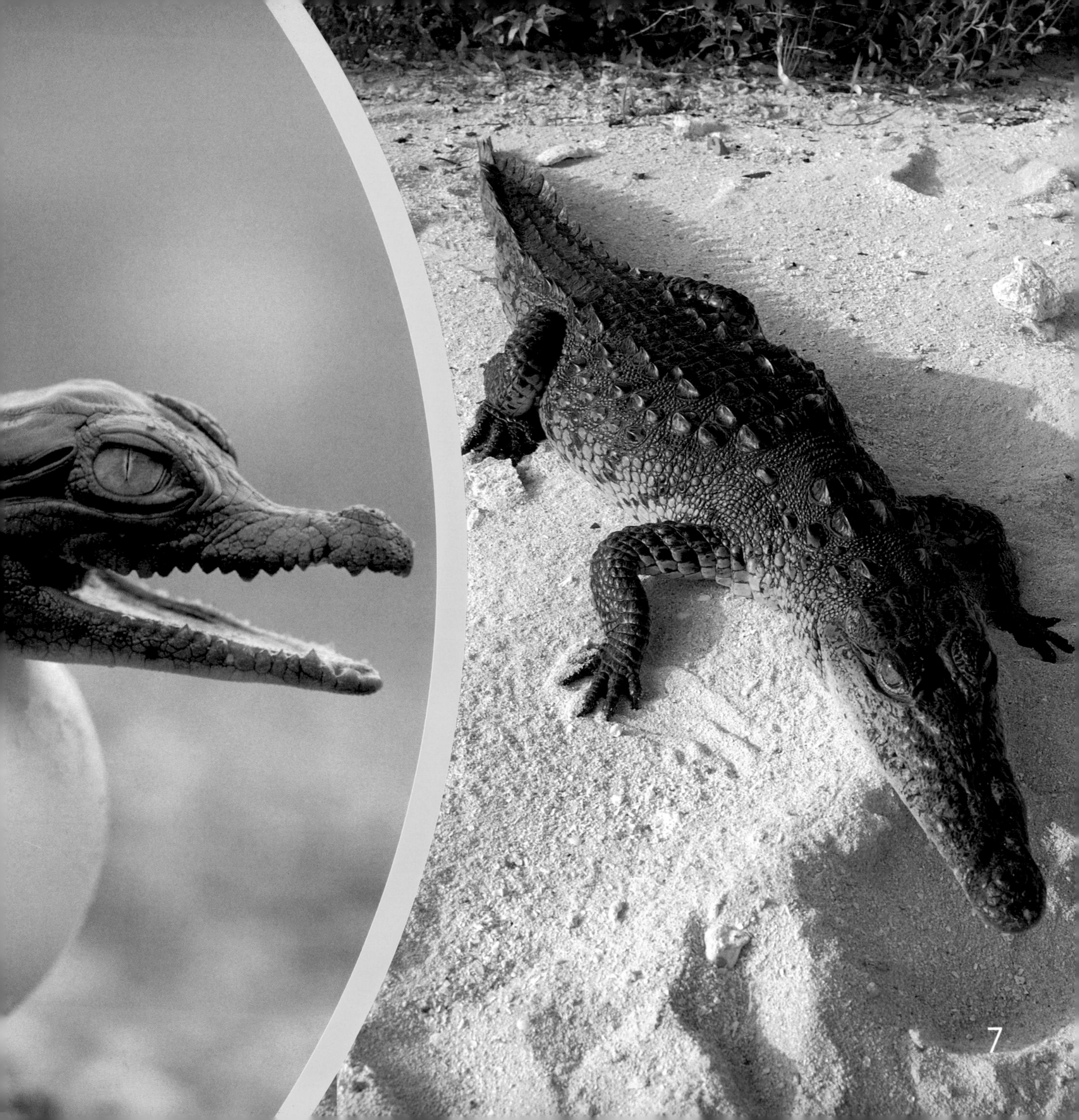

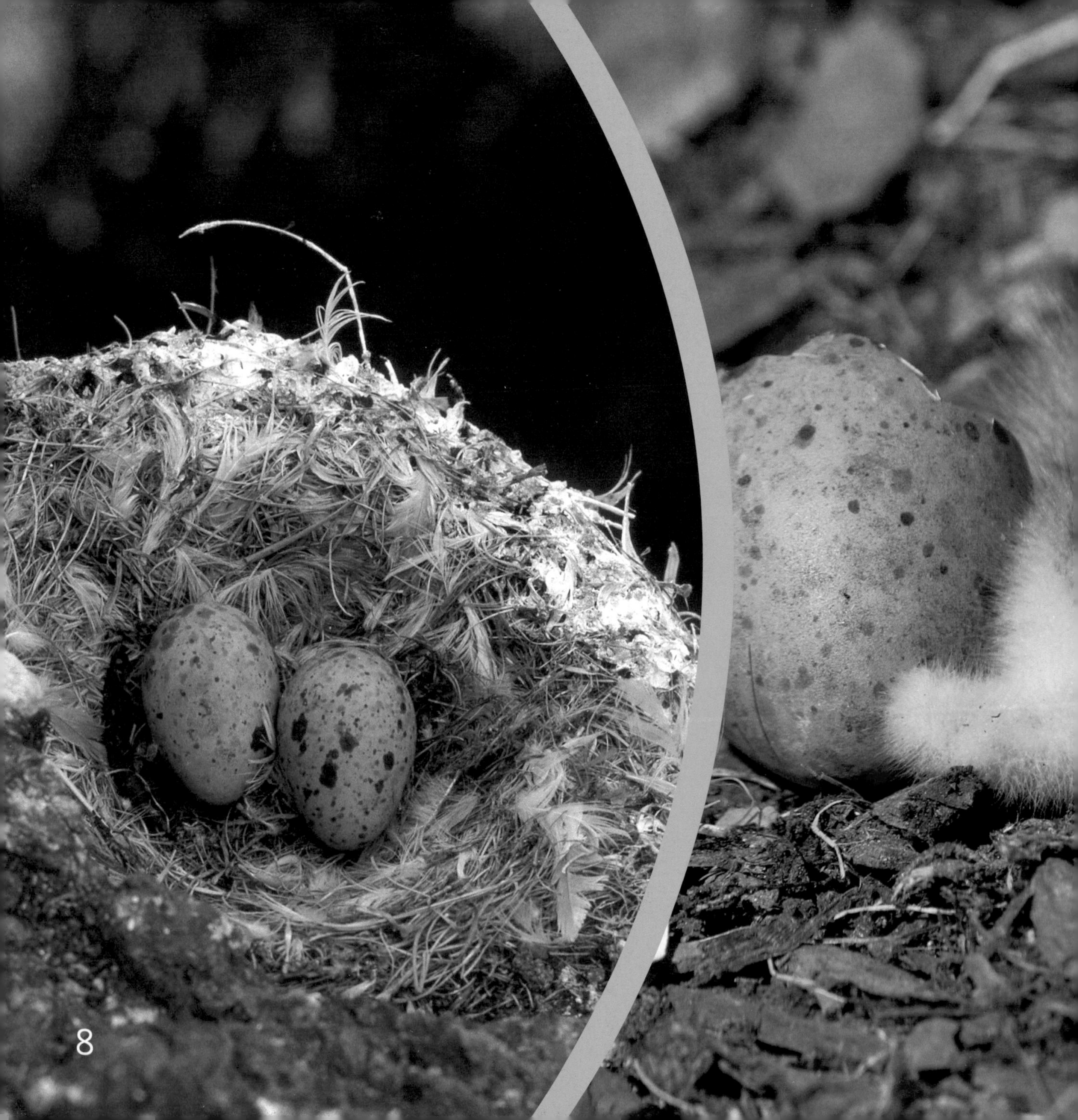

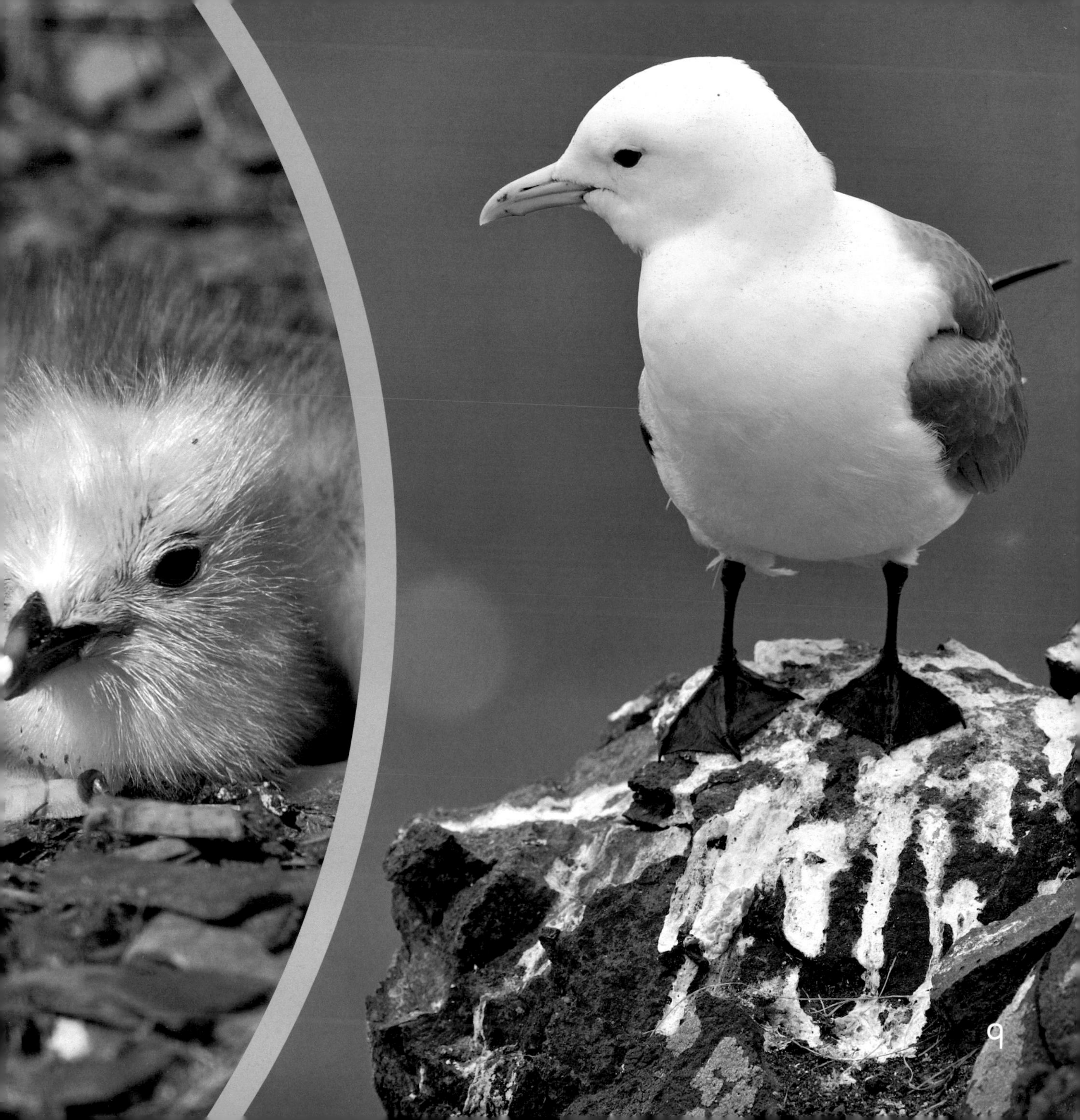

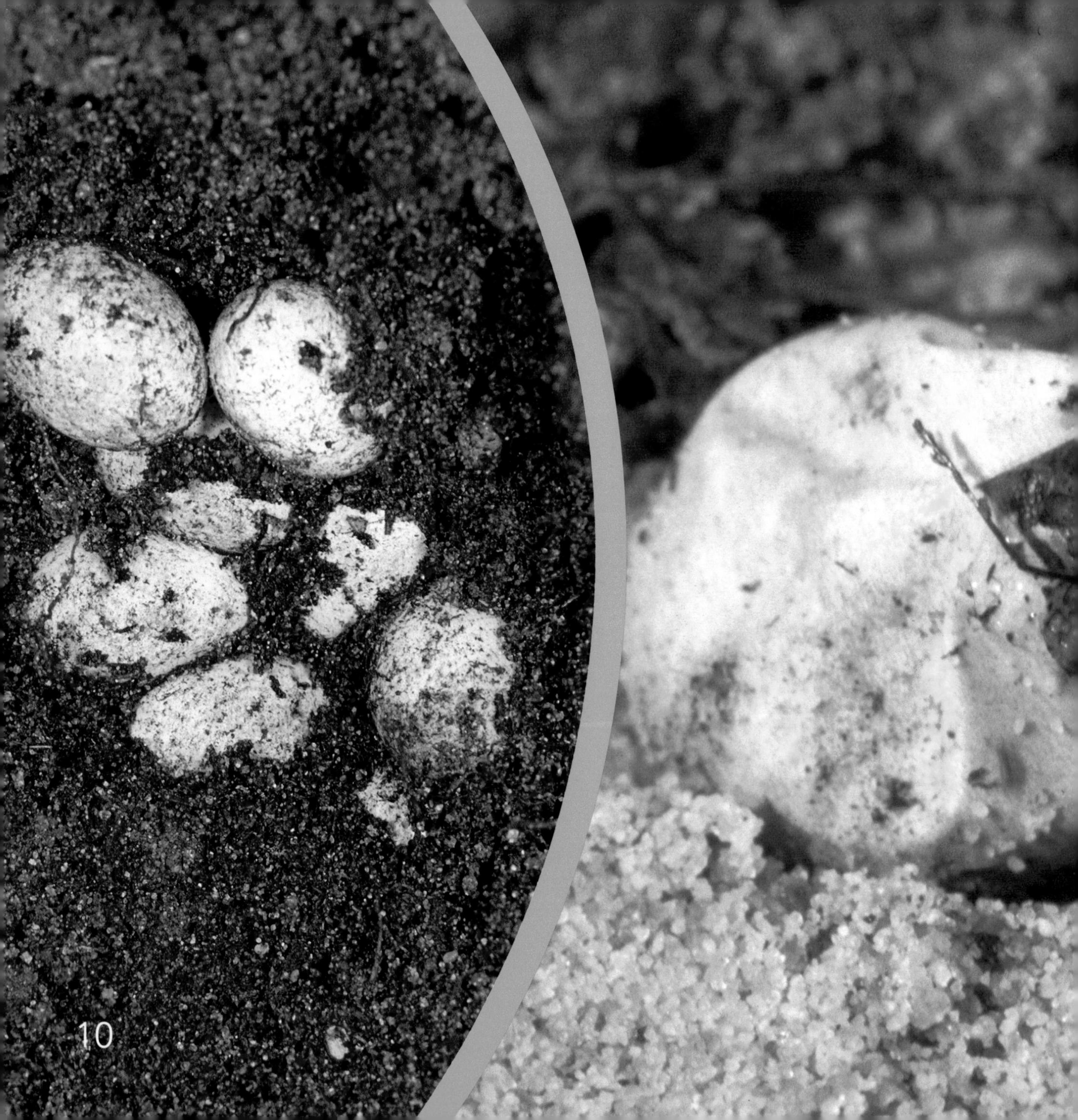

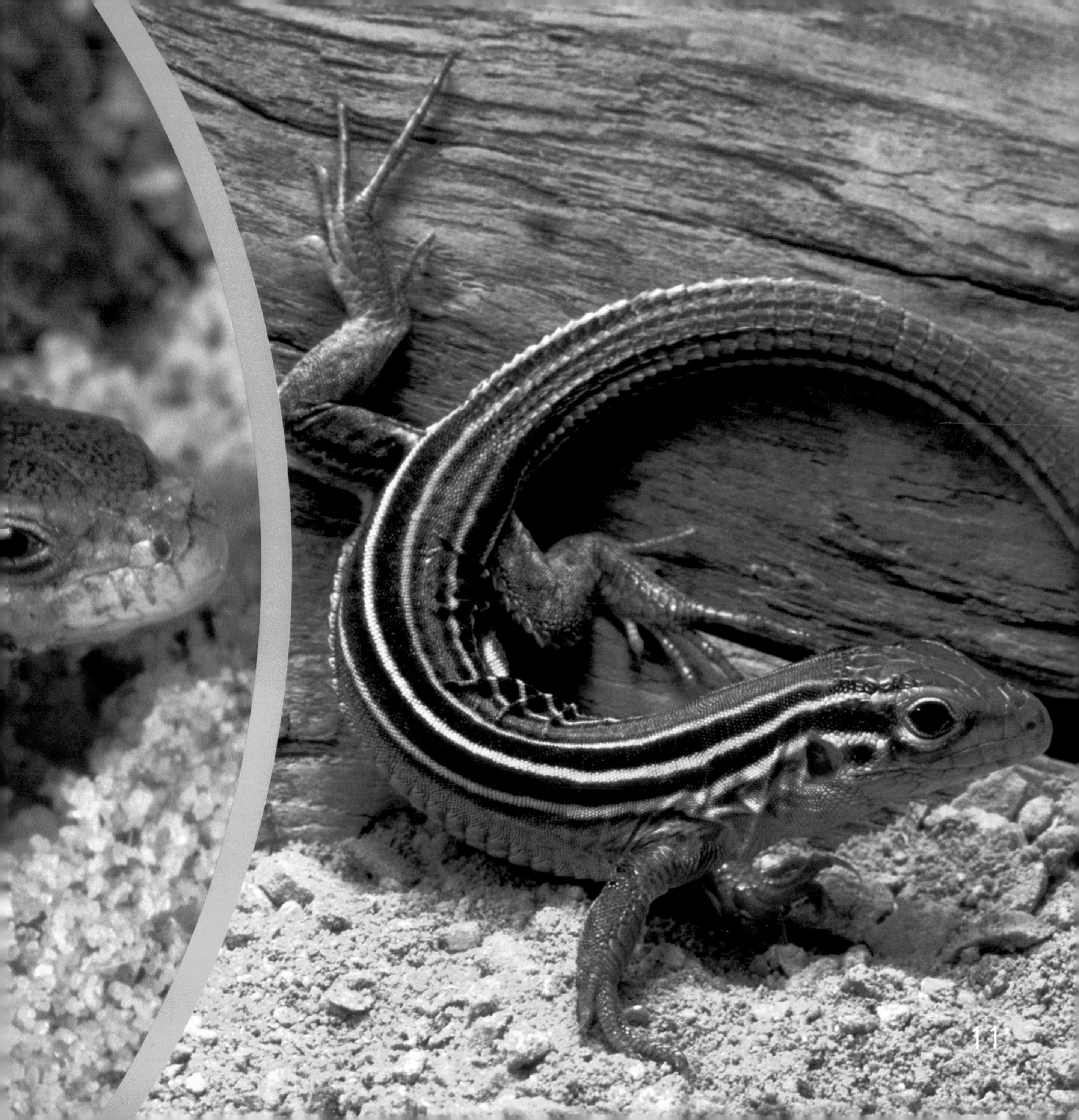

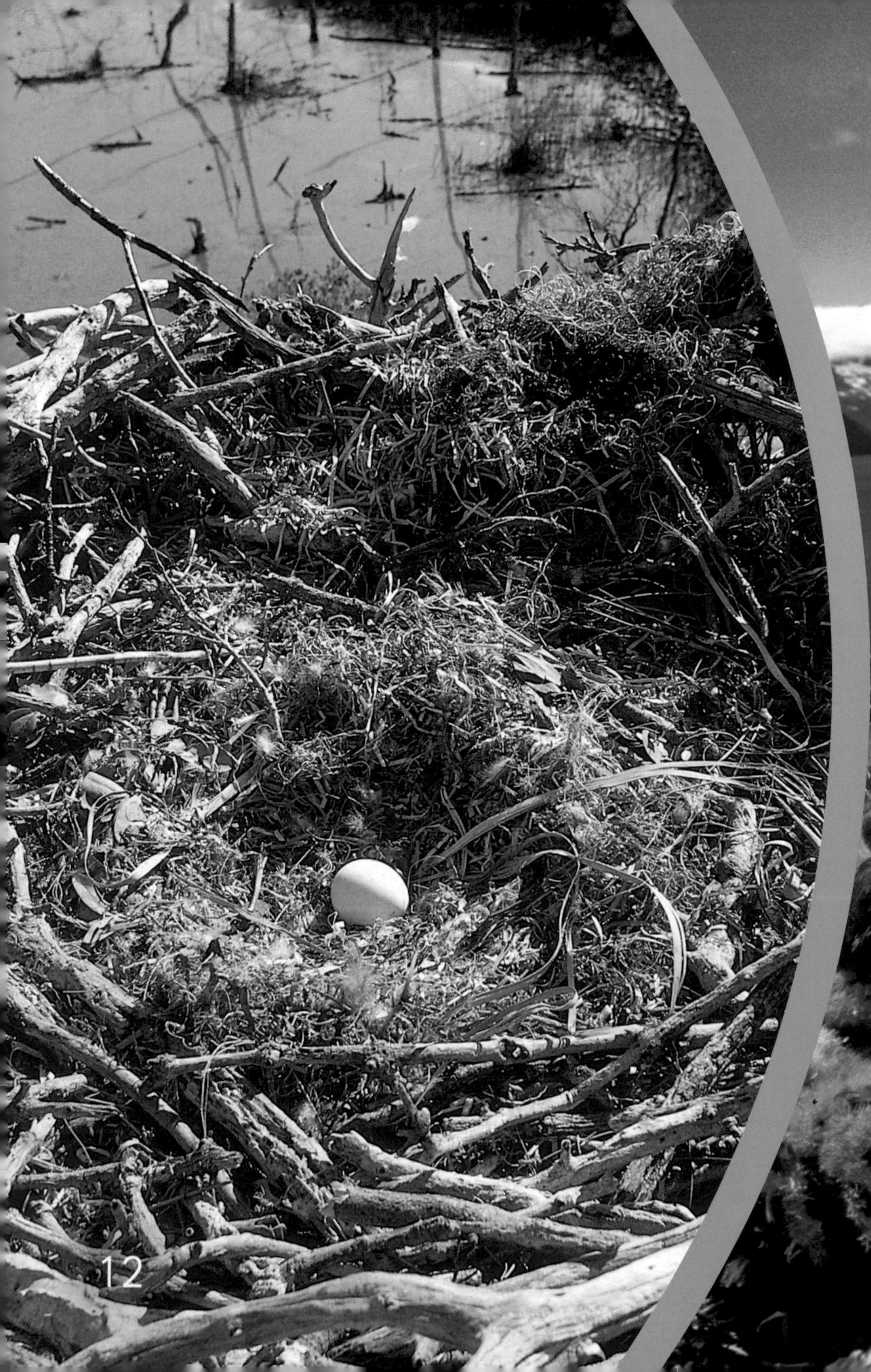
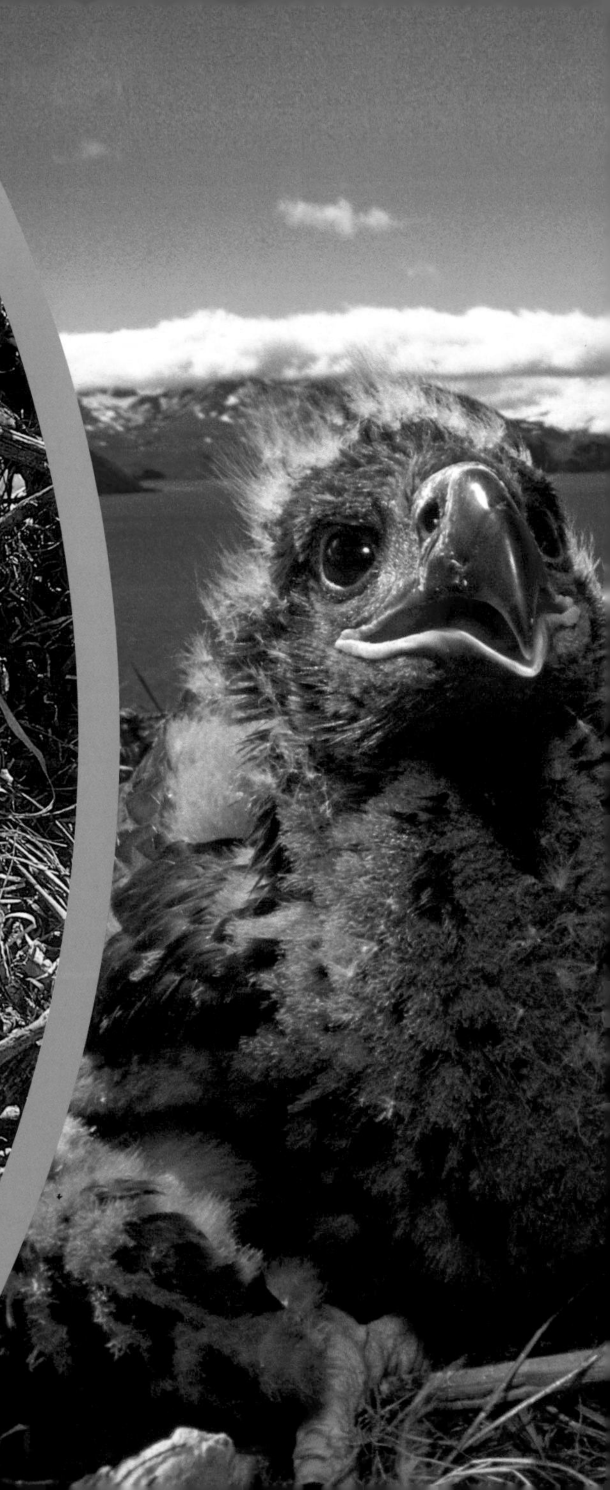

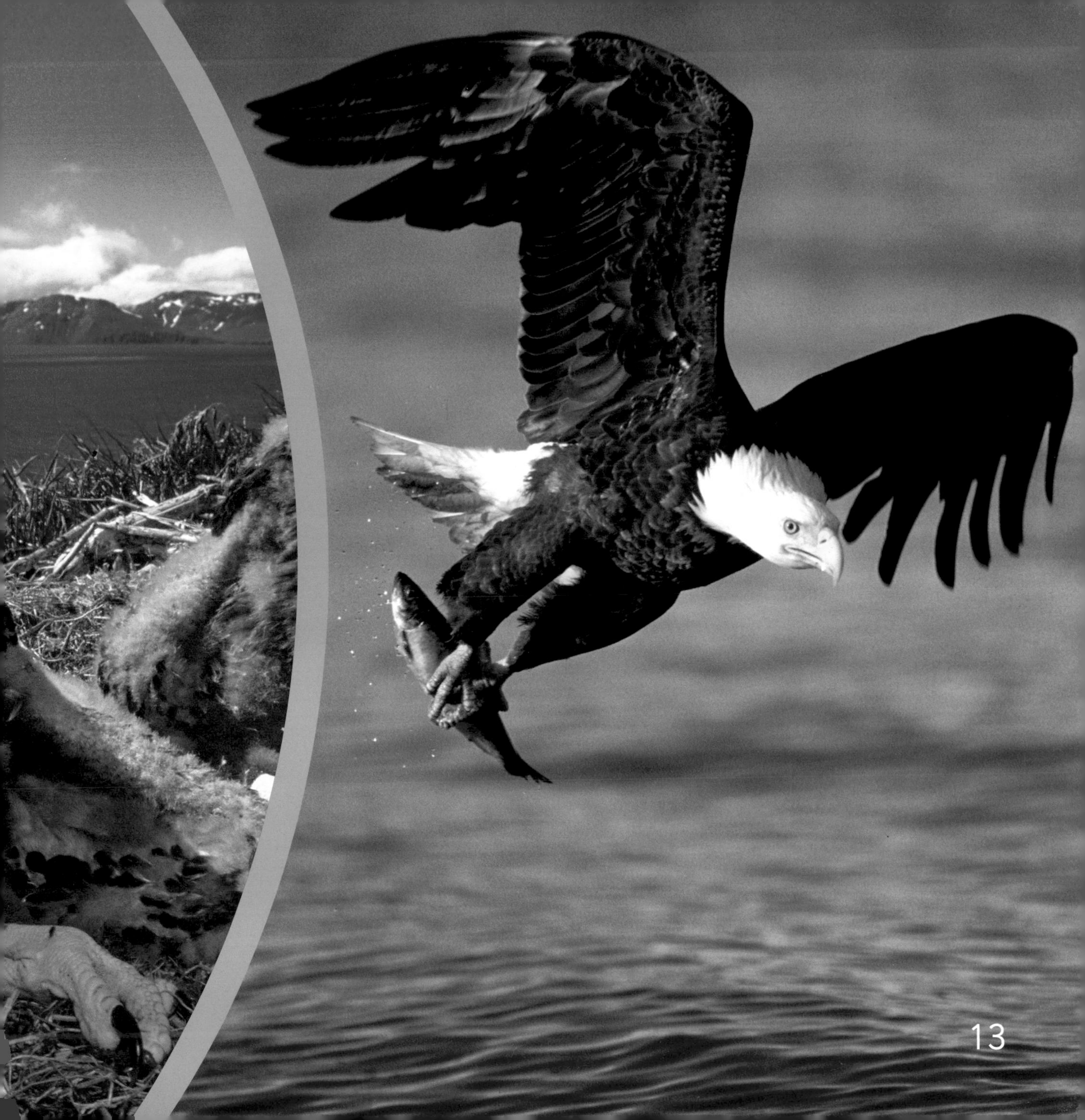

In the eggs

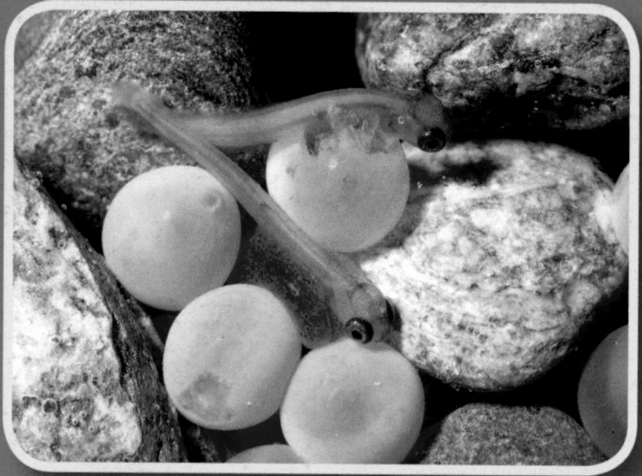

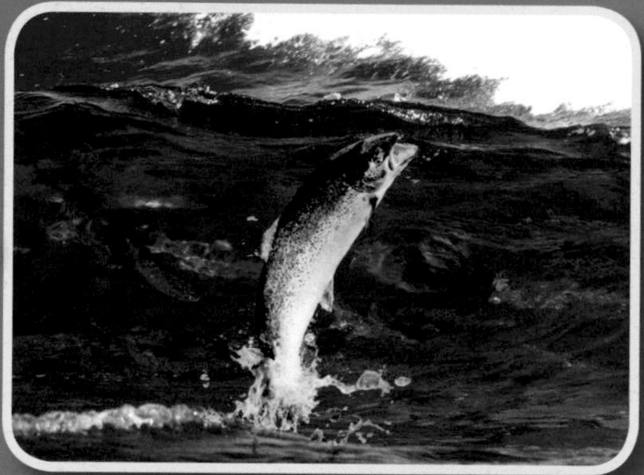

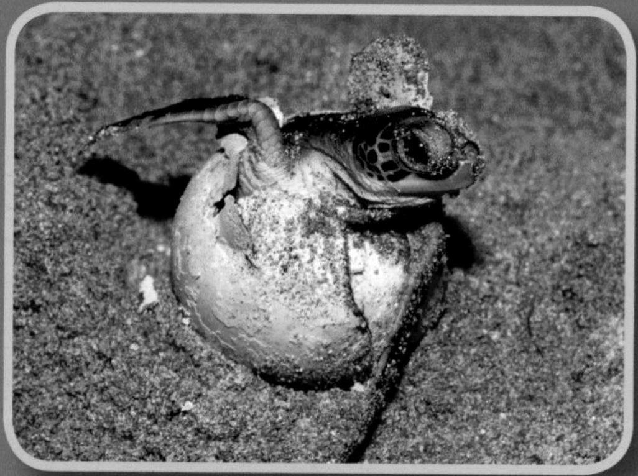

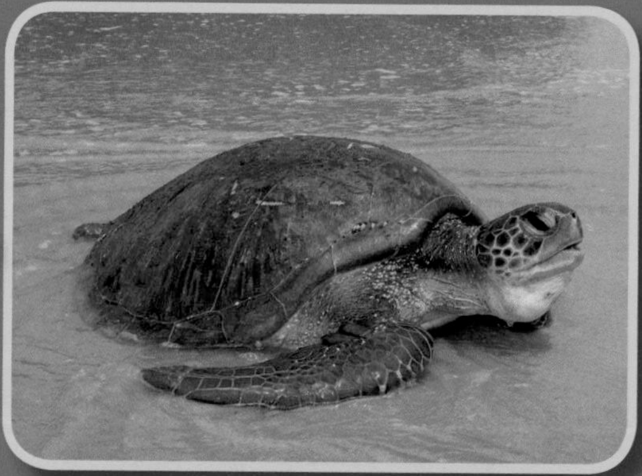

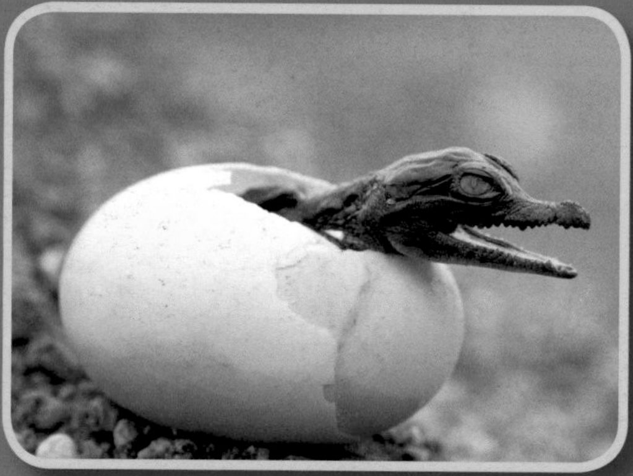

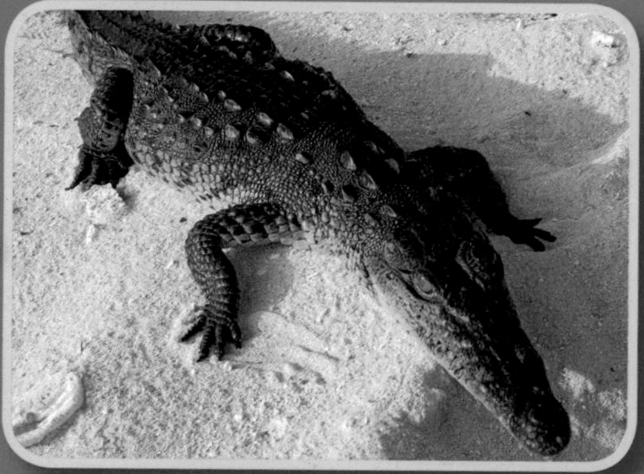